NOTTINGHAMSHIRE

GHOST STORIES

Compiled by Julia Skinner

THE FRANCIS FRITH COLLECTION

www.francisfrith.com

First published in the United Kingdom in 2010 by The Francis Frith Collection®

This edition published exclusively for Bradwell Books in 2013
For trade enquiries see: www.bradwellbooks.com or tel: 0800 834 920
ISBN 978-1-84589-541-9

British Library Cataloguing in Publication Data

Haunted Nottinghamshire - Ghost Stories
Compiled by Julia Skinner

The Francis Frith Collection
6 Oakley Business Park,
Wylye Road, Dinton,
Wiltshire SP3 5EU
Tel: +44 (0) 1722 716 376
Email: info@francisfrith.co.uk
www.francisfrith.com

Printed and bound in Malaysia
Contains material sourced from responsibly managed forests

Front Cover: **NEWARK-ON-TRENT, THE GOVERNOR'S OLD HOUSE 1909** 61804p

The colour-tinting is for illustrative purposes only, and is not intended to be historically accurate

AS WITH ANY HISTORICAL DATABASE, THE FRANCIS FRITH ARCHIVE IS CONSTANTLY BEING
CORRECTED AND IMPROVED, AND THE PUBLISHERS WOULD WELCOME INFORMATION ON
OMISSIONS OR INACCURACIES

CONTENTS

NOTTINGHAM, LONG ROW EAST 1902 48326

HAUNTED NOTTINGHAMSHIRE

The area of Nottingham is believed to have been originally settled in Anglo-Saxon times by the charmlessly-named 'Snot' or 'Snota', and excavations have revealed evidence of early settlement from this period on the eastern of the two hills on which Nottingham stands. Following the Norman Conquest in 1066, William Peverel erected a castle on Tower Rock. It was a naturally impregnable site, with towering cliffs on two sides, and it dominated the country around, including the main road north, which crossed the River Trent below. The castle was steadily added to over the years, and its walls were rebuilt from 1068 onwards. From the mid 12th century it was an important royal castle, and in the 1470s it acquired grand state apartments in the middle bailey. King Charles I raised his standard at Nottingham Castle in 1642, the first action of the Civil War, although he soon left the town, which was strongly pro-Parliament. After the war the bulk of the castle was 'slighted', or rendered useless, by the Parliamentarians in 1651, and reduced to a ruin. Now only the outer bailey east walls and a 14th-century gatehouse of the medieval castle survive, shown in photograph 22843 (opposite) in poor condition prior to being heavily restored in Victorian times. In the 17th century the remains of Nottingham's castle was given to the Duke of Newcastle, who had the upper and middle baileys cleared and levelled in order to build himself a ducal palace. The building appears as austere as a prison block from a distance, but more ornamented when seen from a closer viewpoint. It is now used as a museum and art gallery. Nottingham Castle saw its share of ghastly and dramatic events over the years, one of which took place in 1212, when King John hanged 28 Welsh boy hostages from the castle walls during a Welsh rebellion. The unfortunate youngsters were dragged out one by one to the ramparts to be hanged, and it is said that in the castle precincts you can still hear the pitiful sound of their ghostly pleas for mercy.

**NOTTINGHAM, THE CASTLE
1890** 22848

Did You Know?

Beneath Nottingham's streets is a network of over 400 man-made caves, which visitors can explore on The Caves of Nottingham tour.

NOTTINGHAM, THE CASTLE GATEHOUSE 1890 22843

Photograph 69430 (opposite) shows the ancient Ye Olde Trip to Jerusalem Inn at Nottingham, jutting out of the rock on which Nottingham Castle stands – indeed, it is connected with the myriad sandstone caves just below the castle, and cellars below the inn are carved out of the rock. As the sign outside the inn indicates, the building has been here from at least 1189. This was the year when Richard the Lionheart began the Third Crusade against the Saracens in the Holy Land, and legend has it that knights gathered here before their journey to Jerusalem – hence the inn's name. It is possible that the inn was originally the brewhouse for the castle – the brewing process requires a constant low temperature, which the caves provide; also, two 'chimneys' through the rock lead from the inn to the castle walls, which might have been used in the malting process, or to haul ale from the brewhouse up to the castle. One of these chimneys leads from the Rock Lounge, a room carved out of the rock. Here guests can see the Cursed Galleon, a model of a ship that is said to bring death to anyone who cleans it – so it is shrouded with dust and cobwebs! The parts of the inn outside the rock that we see today date from the middle of the 17th century. Perhaps the most famous landlord at this Nottingham inn has been George Henry Ward, whose popular nickname was 'Yorky' – he was licensee from 1894 to his death in 1914. His ghost is now believed to haunt the cellar caves, where he plays tricks on the inn staff by moving things around.

In the 14th century, Queen Isabella, wife of Edward II, and her lover Sir Roger Mortimer conspired to murder the king and rule as regents during the minority of Isabella and Edward II's son, who became Edward III following his father's death in 1327. When he was 17, the young King Edward III led a coup against his mother and her lover, seized power in his own right and took revenge on his father's killer. On an October night in 1330 the young King Edward III trapped his mother, Queen Isabella, with her lover, Roger Mortimer, at Nottingham Castle, and created one of the castle's most popular and enduring legends – the story of Mortimer's hole. This is a secret tunnel leading from the cellars of Ye Olde Trip to Jerusalem Inn (see photograph 69430, opposite) to the castle, part of the network of caves and subterranean passages beneath Nottingham, through which Edward III and his men crept to capture Isabella and Mortimer whilst they were asleep in their chamber at the castle. Mortimer was conveyed to the Tower of London and later put to death, and his ghost is said to haunt the tunnel to this day.

NOTTINGHAM, YE OLDE TRIP TO JERUSALEM INN
1920 69430

**NOTTINGHAM, WHEELER
GATE 1902** 48327

Photograph 69427 (opposite) shows the Flying Horse Hotel in the centre of Nottingham when it was still in business in the 1920s. This pleasant, rambling old inn, with its beamed ceilings and panelled walls, was a landmark in the city for centuries, and for many years it was where the 'City Fathers' of Nottingham met – one room was known as the Mayor's Parlour. The inn closed for business in the 20th century, and in the 1980s it was converted into a shop, and now forms the entrance to the Flying Horse Walk shopping arcade. The building we see today dates from Elizabethan times, but its massive stone foundations are much older; it is known that in 1400 the site belonged to a medieval charity, the Plumptre Hospital. Below the foundations are ancient caves and passages in two tiers, carved out of the sandstone on which Nottingham stands; how old these are, and why they were created, no-one knows for certain. There were several reports of the building being haunted whilst it was in use as an inn – on one occasion, a man staying there encountered a mysterious 'grey lady' in the corridor near his room and was so scared that he refused to go back into his room, and staff complained that something strange lurked in the beer cellar – when they were in the cellar alone, they experienced an odd sensation of being tapped on their shoulder by an unseen force.

Another of Nottinham's haunted pubs is the Salutation Inn on Maid Marian Way, which has been the scene of many strange happenings over the years, from pint glasses moving along the bar, to levitating ashtrays and glasses falling off the shelves for no obvious reason, often 'floating' some distance away from the shelves before smashing on the floor.

NOTTINGHAM, THE FLYING HORSE HOTEL
1920 69427

NOTTINGHAM, LONG ROW 1890 22815

Nottingham's Galleries of Justice museum in the imposing Shire Hall at High Pavement in the Lace Market area is based in the city's former courthouse and prison, where you can visit the courtrooms and dungeons, sit in the condemned man's cell and find out about crime and punishment in the past. All manner of punishments ranging from whippings and imprisonment to executions once took place here – it is claimed that this was once the only place in Britain where miscreants could be tried, convicted and sentenced, and executions could take place either at the front entrance to the building or in the 'hanging room' if the event was not to be held in public view. The despair and pain that the building has witnessed in the past seems to have left it with a legacy of exceptional paranormal activity, and in 2008 it was voted the UK's most haunted building. When it was visited by Living TV's 'Most Haunted' team in 2003, they reported that it was one of the most terrifying places they had ever investigated; one member of the team claimed to have seen what appeared to be the apparition of a small child, and they picked up apparent poltergeist activity and a number of strange and mysterious noises, including banging and odd 'gurgling' sounds which they traced to the caves beneath the building which were used as dungeons in medieval times – other mediums who have visited the building have also reported the caves as being sites of particularly busy paranormal activity, where stones have been thrown at investigators by an invisible hand, and people have been pushed around by an unseen force. The court room of the Galleries of Justice Museum is also the location for regular sightings of mysterious phenomena – strange black figures have been seen on the balcony, and the sound of screams and groans has also often been reported, perhaps an echo of the reaction of friends and families of the accused when a death sentence was passed here in

former centuries. The bodies of some of the prisoners executed here are buried beneath the flagstones of the Courtyard of the building, which was formerly the prisoners' exercise yard, and strange black misty shadows have been seen here, as well as orbs of light caught on camera. Just off the exercise yard is one of the most horrifying examples of the form that crime and punishment took in the past, a holding cell known as 'the Pitts', which was a hole in the ground, ten feet deep and barred at the top, into which a prisoner would be thrown and left to his fate, and psychic investigators often feel sick and very distressed here. It is claimed that three ghosts haunt the entrance hall of the building, what appears to be a Victorian gentleman who wears a top hat, a soldier and a woman. Many people have reported strange noises in the Cell Corridor, including the rattling of keys, slamming doors and the sound of footsteps pacing along. Strange noises and sounds have also been reported in the Laundry Room, where orbs of light have also been filmed. Staff at the museum in recent years have also taken photos of some very mysterious phenomena – museum caretaker Chris Dole took a photo of what appears to be an apparition of a seated woman in the Sheriff's Dungeons in 2008 and also reported some of his own sightings of odd events, such as witnessing a heavy fire-door opening and closing when no one was there, as if someone invisible was passing through. The Galleries of Justice Museum was also in the news in March 2010, when Simon Brown, a qualified parapsychologist from Peterborough, took a photo which showed a mysterious figure even though there was no one else around at the time. The figure appeared to be wearing the clothing of a late 19th-century prisoner, and its right leg seemed to be dragging a chain. The figure appears transparent in the photo, and the bars on the window behind it can be seen through the apparition.

NOTTINGHAM, LONG ROW EAST
1890 22814

NOTTINGHAM, WOLLATON HALL 1928 81579

The tide of Nottingham's expansion has now swept round Wollaton House, one of the great Elizabethan houses. Designed by Robert Smithson for Sir Francis Willoughby, who made his fortune from coal, it was built in the 1580s and is set in 500 acres of park. The land was bought by the Corporation in 1925. There have been a number of reports of strange happenings at Wollaton Hall. Many attendants at the Hall have felt the temperature suddenly drop, or been aware of a hostile presence, often accompanied by the sound of a door slamming, footsteps, creaking floorboards and groans, particularly in Room 19, now used as an exhibition area. Investigations have found that Room 19 was where Lady Middleton was confined in her later years, in great pain after an accident in which she fell down some stairs. The area outside the Hall also seems to be haunted, as strange lights have been seen around the dovecote and the stable yard, and the ghost of a woman walking her dog has sometimes been seen around the lake.

On the outskirts of Nottingham is Clifton Hall, which hit the national news headlines in 2008 as the location of a terrifying sequence of events. The present house is a handsome edifice that was mainly built between 1778 to 1797, designed by John Carr of York, but it stands on the former site of a fortified tower house that was built here in the 13th century for the Clifton family, the lords of the manor. Clifton Hall was sold away from the Clifton family in 1958 and it became Clifton Hall Girls' Grammar School, which remained open until 1976 during which time there were rumours of the hall being haunted. It was then used by Trent Polytechnic (now Nottingham Trent University) until 2002, when it was sold and converted into two luxury apartments. The house was then bought by a wealthy businessman, Anwar Rashid, in January 2007, who moved into it with his family. Eight months later Mr Rashid and his family fled the building, claiming that it was haunted, and were so desperate to get rid of the property that they handed it back to their bank, losing a considerable amount of money as a result. Mr Rashid claimed that paranormal activity in Clifton Hall had terrified the family from the first day they moved in; the phenomena included the sounds of screaming in the corridors, mysterious figures which appeared in the shape of their children even though they were elsewhere in the house at the time, knocking noises on walls and a ghostly man's voice asking "Is anybody there?" even though there was no one else in the house, and all the doors and windows were locked and closed. Other strange events convinced the family that there was something unnatural in the hall and they called in Ashfield Paranormal Investigation Network to help; the group's leader reported back that they had found their investigation to be a truly frightening experience, but they were unable to do anything to put a stop to the paranormal activity. The last straw came for the Rashid family when they were horrified to find unexplained drops of blood on their baby's bedding, and they moved out of the hall that day. Mr Rashid was reported in the media comparing the family's experience to the events in the feature film 'The Others', describing is as: "We were like the family in 'The Others'. The ghosts didn't want us to be there and we could not fight them because we couldn't see them."

Close to Clifton Hall near Nottingham is the wooded area of Clifton Grove, on a cliff overlooking the River Trent. According to legend, this was the site of a suicide in medieval times, when a young woman jumped off the cliff into the river. Some tales say that she killed herself in despair because she had been jilted by her lover, but others say that it was she who had been unfaithful, and that her brokenhearted sweetheart threw himself to his death in the river here first, and that the woman killed herself the same way soon afterward, overcome with guilt for her betrayal of his love. Her remorseful ghost has been said to haunt the area ever since.

The town of Arnold is now a suburb of Nottingham, to the north-east of the city boundary. The Bonington Theatre in Arnold's Leisure Centre is famously haunted by a restless spirit that is affectionately known as 'Edna'. The sound of footsteps is often heard from inside the theatre after it has been locked up at night, doors mysteriously open when no one is there, unexplained 'cold spots' are felt around the building for no obvious reason, objects are found in a different place from that where they have been left, and lights are switched on by an unseen hand. There is a tradition that the building was erected on land which was formerly a Quaker burial site, and that the ghost is the disturbed shade of someone who was interred there – perhaps the woman whose skull and bones were found on the site during the building's construction in the 1980s. Although some staff are unnerved by the ghostly activity, the phenomenon has been investigated by several clairvoyants who have reported that the ghost is friendly and harmless.

NOTTINGHAM, RIVER TRENT BENEATH CLIFTON GROVE 1893 33253

A particularly haunted location near Nottingham is the village of Calverton. The Admiral Rodney public house is said to be haunted by the restless spirit of Tom Shadwell, who was the innkeeper here in the mid 19th century. Another former member of staff who haunts the cellars of the pub is 'Sarah', thought be the shade of a serving girl who worked at the inn who now amuses herself with a little light poltergeist activity. The sound of ghostly children playing around the pub has also been reported. Ghostly activity in the village which is more frightening occurs in the George's Lane and George's Hill areas of Calverton, where a mysterious apparition has been reported which materialises on the back seat of passing cars in both locations, although it seems to take two different forms – on George's Lane it appears as an old lady, and on George's Hill it is more sinister, showing as a figure dressed in a black hooded robe, or a black hat. Witnesses who have seen both apparitions have only glimpsed them on the back seat of their vehicle in the rear view mirror as they drive along – when they turn round to see what is there, the figure has disappeared… A phantom woman is also said to stand beside the road near Old Hall Close.

For more fascinating accounts of ghostly activity in Calverton, see the village website: www.calvertonvillage.com

SOUTHWELL, MARKET PLACE c1960 S564026

Photograph S564026 (above) shows the Saracen's Head in the attractive minster town of Southwell. Since this photograph was taken, the stucco which had been applied in 1693 to the first floor has been stripped off to reveal the timber-framing beneath. It was from this 16th-century timber-framed inn during the Civil War that Charles I ordered the town of Newark-on-Trent to surrender to the Parliamentarians in May 1646, as part of his attempted negotiations with the Scottish army encamped at Kelham, and it was in this inn that Charles I spent his last night of freedom before himself surrendering to the Scots to be handed over to the Parliamentary forces and taking his first steps on the path that would eventually end with his execution in 1649. At the time of Charles I's stay the inn was known as the King's Head; the name was changed to the Saracen's Head in 1651, according to local tradition because it was believed that Charles I had been beheaded with a Saracen sword which had come to England during the Crusades. The phantom of the ill-fated king is now reputed to haunt the King Charles Suite in the oldest part of what is now the Saracen's Head Hotel. The shades of a man and a woman dressed in 18th-century fashion are also said to roam the building.

SOUTHWELL, WESTGATE 1920 69469

The ghost of a bearded man who has been nicknamed 'Ballroom Charlie' haunts the Admiral Rodney Hotel in Southwell, seen on the right of photograph 69472 (opposite). The apparition has been seen by several of the pub's landlords over the years, and is most often spotted staring back at you reflected in the glass doors to the old ballroom. It is also responsible for occasional poltergeist activity, playing tricks on staff and customers. Ghostly activity has also been reported at the Bramley Apple pub in Church Street in the town, where something in the cellar regularly interferes with the flow of the liquid refreshment from the barrels to the bar. The Bramley Apple pub is named after the popular cooking apple which originates from Southwell, which holds an annual Bramley Apple Festival. The first tree grew from pips planted in her cottage garden in 1809 by a little girl called Mary Ann Brailing; the cottage and garden was bought by a Southwell butcher, Matthew Bramley, in 1846, and ten years later a local nurseryman called Henry Merryweather asked permission to take cuttings from the apple tree to produce apple trees commercially – Mr Bramley gave permission, but on condition that the apple from the trees should be named after him.

The ghost of a young woman called Elizabeth Shepherd is said to haunt Harlow Wood, near Mansfield, around the spot where she was murdered in 1817 by a scissor-grinder, Charles Rotherham, who attacked her with a wooden stake whilst she was making her way to Mansfield to seek work. Rotherham was apprehended a few days later when he tried to sell Elizabeth's shoes in an inn at Redhill, and was hanged at Nottingham. There is a memorial stone to Elizabeth on the A60, about half a mile north of the junction with the B6020 Kirkby road, and her ghost is said to appear whenever the stone is moved. The inscription on the stone reads: 'This stone is erected to the memory of Elizabeth Shepherd, of Papplewick, who was murdered while passing this spot by Charles Rotherham, July 17th, 1817. Aged 17 years.'

SOUTHWELL, KING STREET 1920 69472

MANSFIELD, THE MARKET PLACE c1955 M184034

Mansfield 103.2 FM is an independent local radio station based at the Brunts Business Centre at Mansfield. It seems that there is a ghost in the building where the radio station is based which has media ambitions – at precisely 8.00am on 28th July 2008, newsreader Ian Watkins was in the studio preparing for the 8.00am news when he heard a voice on air whispering 'Time' just after the news jingle had been played – but there was no one else present in the studio at the time. Watkins heard the voice so clearly that it stopped him beginning his news bulletin. The only explanation that could be given was that it might have been a ghostly echo of the voice of a teacher from the building's past, when it was the old Brunts School building, part of a charitable establishment set up by Samuel Brunts, a wealthy former resident of Mansfield who died in 1711 leaving most of his wealth for charitable purposes, including a bequest left for the education of poor boys. There is a statue of Samuel Brunts on the corner of the Brunts Charity Building on the corner of Leeming Street and Toothill Lane in Mansfield, which was built in 1915.

A few miles from Mansfield is the Pleasley Vale Business Park where the old Pleasley Vale Mills complex of three buildings can be found. Pleasley Vale Mills, originally a cotton spinning mill, was built in 1784 by Henry Hollins and four business colleagues, and became a major local employer. In the late 19th century the business at Pleasley Vale Mills trademarked 'Viyella' branded fabric – a mixture of Merino wool and cotton which was both soft and durable – which became very popular for the manufacture of women's wear. The firm became Coats Viyella in 1967. The Pleasley Vale Mills factory closed in 1987 and the buildings have now been renovated and adapted for use by small businesses and other purposes. Working conditions at the mills for both adults and children in the late 18th and 19th centuries were not good, and there is a tale that an upper floor of one of the mill buildings is haunted by the distraught ghost of a woman worker who was raped and killed here by a cruel supervisor. The Pleasley Vale Mills site is said to be haunted by a number of other apparitions, one of which is a ghostly man often spotted outside the buildings and who appears so real that people have walked over to speak to him. A shadowy lady dressed in black clothing has also been seen, who appears to walk through walls, and a spectral man is said to haunt the old Dye Room, or walk from the old Dye House to Mill Number Two.

MANSFIELD, MARKET PLACE c1950 M184028

Newstead Abbey, 12 miles north of Nottingham, was an Augustinian priory founded in the 1160s which was dissolved by Henry VIII and granted to the Byron family in 1539, who converted the former abbey buildings into a stately home. The house envelopes much of the former abbey cloisters and the buildings surrounding them, and the great 13th-century abbey west front survives. There is a legend that when the last abbot of Newstead Abbey was forced to surrender the abbey to the king's men, he

LORD BYRON 1788-1824 A001087

placed a curse on the buildings, and on all those who would live there in later years. Since then, Newstead Abbey has been said to be haunted by several ghosts, including that of a Black Friar (who became known as the 'Goblin Friar') whose appearances always herald disaster for the owners of the house – the apparition appears dressed in a black habit, with a skull beneath its hood instead of a face. Also, the rooks that nest in the trees near the building are said to be the souls of long dead monks that are still watching over the place.

Newstead Abbey was inherited by the 'mad, bad and dangerous to know' poet Lord Byron in 1798, and he lived there for a short time. Lord Byron himself claimed to have seen the ghost of the 'Goblin Monk' before embarking on his disastrous marriage to Annabella Millbank in 1815 and referred to the legend in his poem 'Don Juan':

"With steps that trod as heavy, yet unheard; His garments only a slight murmur made; He moved as shadowy as the sisters weird". After Lord Byron's death in Greece in 1824 his body was brought back and buried in the family vault at Hucknall's parish church, four miles south of Newstead Abbey. The house and its 300 acres of park were presented to the City of Nottingham in 1931, and major collections of Byron memorabilia are now displayed in the house. Another spectre which haunts the grounds of Newstead Abbey is believed to be the shade of Sophie Hyatt, a shy, deaf girl who lived in the area in the early 19th century, who was obsessed with Lord Byron and a great fan of his poetry. After his death she took to roaming the grounds crying 'Alas, my Lord Byron!'; she became known as 'The Little White Lady of Newstead' because she was always dressed in light, white clothing. She was tragically killed in an accident in 1825, run over by a horse and cart. A path in the part of the gardens where her still-grieving ghost is said to be seen particularly often is now known as White Lady's Walk.

NEWSTEAD ABBEY, FROM THE WEST 1890 22856

WORKSOP,
THE PRIORY
GATEHOUSE
c1938
W278057

Worksop is the largest town in north Nottinghamshire. The town's finest building is the Priory of Our Lady and St Cuthbert, formerly known as Radford Priory. The medieval town was at its gates, but moved northwards to its present location. The priory was founded c1120 for Augustinian canons (known as the Black Canons, after the hooded black cloaks they wore over a black cassock). The present nave dates from the later 12th century, and of the priory's east end only the superb Lady Chapel survives. The transepts with their two storeys of arches date from the 1920s and 1930s, while a modern central tower with a slender spire and a choir was erected from 1966 to 1974 by Laurence King. Of the priory buildings, only the mid 14th-century gatehouse survives, shown in photograph W278057 (above). A ghostly apparition known as 'the Blue Lady' dressed in a long medieval-style gown is said to haunt the grounds of the priory, walking from the gatehouse to the church before vanishing into thin air, but Worksop Priory is particularly famous for the ghostly form which is seen on the roof of the priory church – sometimes the apparition is assumed to be the same 'Blue Lady', but other reports of it describe it as a man, and it is probably a ghostly monk. He only appears late at night, usually between 1am and 4am, and appears to be very agitated, or perhaps very frightened, jumping around on the top of one of the two towers of the church and cautiously peering over the wall at something only he can see, before fading away.

WORKSOP, BRIDGE STREET 1967 W278093

WORKSOP, THE PRIORY CHURCH c1955 W278053

Retford (officially known as East Retford) has at its heart a market place, first chartered in 1246. Until the A1 bypassed the town in the 1960s the Great North Road from London to Edinburgh streamed along its east side. Ironically, the old Great North Road had been diverted in 1766 so that East Retford could benefit economically from the coaching trade and commerce, while the Chesterfield Canal further boosted the town's prosperity, as did the coming of the railway in the 19th century. This prosperity was demonstrated in the building of a new Town Hall in the 1860s, seen in photograph R261044 (opposite) with its clock tower. A ghostly figure dressed in a black gown and wearing a grey wig is reputed to haunt the main staircase of the Town Hall – from his dress, he is assumed to be the unquiet shade of a judge from the period of the early 20th century, but it is not known who he is, or why he lurks here. In 1975 he was seen by both a cleaner at the Town Hall and also by the town clerk, both of whom were so convinced that they had seen something uncanny that they reported it to the BBC radio programme 'Down Your Way' when it came to Retford in 1978.

One of Retford's old coaching inns, the White Hart Hotel, is said to be haunted by the ghost of a young girl who was killed in a coach accident at the rear of the building and whose spirit still lingers around the place where she met her death. Her footsteps have been heard walking along empty corridors in the hotel. Another haunted hotel in the area is the West Retford Hotel, a few miles west of Retford, where the ghost of an unfaithful wife roams the corridors and leaves the building to go across the courtyard to where the stables used to be. It is said that in the early 1900s she lived in the building and had an illicit affair with the stable boy, who killed himself in shame when their affair became public knowledge. The fate of the woman herself is not known, but perhaps her unquiet shade is doomed to walk eternally because of the remorse she felt.

RETFORD, MARKET PLACE c1955   R261044

Newark-on-Trent grew up where the Fosse Way, the Roman road from Axminster in Devon to Lincoln, met the medieval Great North Road's predecessor and crossed the River Trent. The name is Danish, meaning 'new fortress', and the strategic importance of the river crossing defended by river cliffs is emphasised by Newark's castle. The streets and lanes of the town are still mostly as laid out by Alexander the Magnificent, Bishop of Lincoln in the early 12th century. At the heart of Bishop Alexander's town was the large market place into which the Fosse Way was diverted. Newark enjoyed great prosperity in the 18th century through industrial growth and through its status as a coaching town on the Great North Road. There was much rebuilding then, so the town has a predominately Georgian character; there was further rebuilding after the railway, the east coast main line, arrived in the 1840s. There are many ghosts around Newark, and the town's Millgate Museum in a former Victorian warehouse on the banks of the River Trent is itself a haunted building. A ghostly man dragging a chain attached to his leg is said to hobble down Albert Street from time to time, and the Old King's Arms pub at Kirk Gate is

the favourite local of a poltergeist nicknamed 'Stomper' because of the loud stomping noises that accompany his activity; amongst his tricks, he opens doors or slams them shut, and is blamed for furniture being mysteriously moved around. Newark's Palace Theatre on Appleton Gate also seems to have a resident ghost who opens and closes doors as if he is passing through them, and whose footsteps have been heard pacing around the empty building at night.

NEWARK-ON-TRENT, KIRKGATE 1900 45106

NEWARK-ON-TRENT, MARKET PLACE 1890 24655

NEWARK-ON-TRENT, APPLETON GATE 1906 56498

The castle at Newark-on-Trent was started by Alexander, Bishop of Lincoln in the 1130s, but much of what we see now is 14th-century (see photograph N12081, opposite). Once known as 'the Key to the North', the strategically important castle had a chequered history – King John died here in 1216, and in the Civil War of the 17th century the staunchly Royalist town of Newark-on-Trent and its castle endured three long sieges – in 1642, 1644 and 1646. Indeed, the town had extensive defensive earthworks all around it, with bastions for artillery pieces. Similarly, the besieging Parliamentarian forces threw up earthworks. Many of these remain, including The Queen's Sconce, an impressively complete earthwork battery in Devon Park; the Hawton Redoubt, south of the town; Sandhill Sconce; and others south of the Muskham Bridge. Such a complete picture of a 17th-century siege is very rare. After the Civil War the castle was ordered to be demolished, but fortunately the long walls to the river front and half of the east wall largely survived. Newark Castle has been visited regularly by paranormal investigators looking into the busy supernatural activity which has been reported here over the years. The strange phenomena witnessed by staff working at the castle include lights and computer equipment seeming to mysteriously switch themselves on, strange lights being seen in some rooms, objects being moved by unseen hands, and mysterious voices being heard on radios. On one occasion when a group from Northern Ghost Research Investigation Team UK was conducting its investigations at the castle, a tennis ball was thrown at the team – from an empty room. Most of the paranormal activity is said to emanate from the south-west tower, the north tower and the undercroft – where the NGRIT-UK team sensed the presence of the spirit of an insane woman. Unsurprisingly in view of its role in the Civil War, the shades of soldiers from that conflict are also reputed to roam the building.

NEWARK-ON-TRENT, THE CASTLE c1965 N12081

**NEWARK-ON-TRENT,
FROM TRENT BRIDGE
1909** 61796

Stodman Street in Newark-on-Trent is where the famous Governor's House can be found, a 16th-century timber-framed house with three storeys of coved jetties (see photograph 61804, opposite) which is now used as a bakery. It has survived relatively unchanged because of its historical associations with the Civil War; it was the residence of Sir Richard Willis, the Royalist governor during the war, and a plaque informs us that King Charles I's nephew, the dashing cavalry leader Prince Rupert, stayed here in 1645. This atmospheric building is said to be the home of something uncanny – in the 1990s the sound of unexplained footsteps was heard in the attic, and the building was permeated by the scent of violets, for no reason that could be found.

NEWARK-ON-TRENT, SHOPS IN STODMAN STREET 1906 56494x

NEWARK-ON-TRENT, THE GOVERNOR'S OLD HOUSE 1909 61804

NEWARK-ON-TRENT, YE OLDE WHITE HART c1955 N12006

In the south-east corner of Newark-on-Trent's Market Square is its only surviving timber-framed building, Ye Olde White Hart, a superb and rich example of late 15th-century building (see photograph N12006, above). Dilapidated for some years, it has now been beautifully restored, with the timber painted in many colours as an authentic reconstruction of a medieval colour scheme. The cellars of this ancient pub are said to be haunted by a supernatural entity…

On the outskirts of Newark is the large village of Balderton. Its parish church of St Giles dates from the 12th-century and is said to be haunted by a ghostly woman known as 'Jane', and it may also be her entity that has been spotted on some occasions gliding around the area of the church late at night.

BALDERTON, THE VILLAGE 1909 61813

Ye Olde Bell Hotel at Barnby Moor was described in the 18th century as a 'gentleman-like, comfortable house'; it has some fine rooms, including the one seen in photograph B607014 (below) with panelling and a Jacobean-style plaster ceiling, all Victorian. The hotel is said to be haunted by a 'Grey Lady', a wraith-like entity that glides along the corridors and the staircase of the building, and has also been seen in the ballroom. A mysterious ghostly man has also been seen on occasions going into one of the rooms of the hotel – but then, upon investigation, the room has been found to be empty…

BARNBY MOOR, THE WISETON ROOM, YE OLDE BELL HOTEL c1955 B607014

BARNBY MOOR, YE OLDE BELL HOTEL c1955 B607009

The magnificent Thoresby Hall at Ollerton, now the Thoresby Hall Hotel, has been the subject of investigation by NGRIT-UK (Northern Ghost Research and Investigation Team) for many years. An incredible number of strange phenomena at the hotel have been recorded by both the NGRIT-UK team and by the hotel staff, including the unnerving sound of whispering voices, strange banging and knocking noises, the sound of footsteps pacing along the empty corridors, and objects and furniture being thrown around or mysteriously moved. The restaurant in the former wine cellar of the hall is said to be haunted by a ghostly dog, a favourite pet of a former resident at some time in the past, and phantom children are said to play in the garden. The Great Hall is on the first floor and three storeys high: a truly monumental space with galleries overlooking the hall. The figure of a strange lady dressed in black has been spotted staring down into the Great Hall from the gallery. The view of the Great Hall shown in photograph O131042 (right) shows it as it appeared in the mid 1950s, when it was still a private home for the last Earl Manvers, who died in 1955.

OLLERTON, THORESBY HALL
c1955 O131028

OLLERTON, THORESBY HALL, THE GREAT HALL c1955 O131042

In the Rufford Abbey Country Park near Ollerton stand the ruins of the medieval Rufford Abbey, said to be one of Nottinghamshire's most haunted sites. The Cistercian abbey was dissolved in 1536 and the land and abbey buildings became part of a country house estate which was owned first by the Talbot and later the Savile families. Rufford Abbey was bought by Nottinghamshire County Council as a crumbling ruin in the 1950s and efforts were made to consolidate the structure, but sadly the large early 18th-century block of the building seen in photograph O1331016 (opposite) had to be demolished in 1956. Nowadays there is an interesting monastic exhibition in the Undercroft of Rufford Abbey ruins, but sharp-eyed visitors may glimpse another relic from its medieval past – the abbey ruins are said to be haunted by a giant ghostly monk, with a skull beneath the cowl of his habit instead of a face. Ghost hunters might prefer to give this one a miss though – an early parish register for the nearby village of Edwinstowe records the burial of a man who 'died of fright from seeing the Rufford ghost'.

In the extreme north of Nottinghamshire is Scrooby. Now bypassed by heavy traffic, in former centuries Scrooby was situated on a major turnpiked road, and there was a tollkeeper's house just outside the village. In 1779 one John Spencer murdered the tollkeeper and his wife whilst attempting to steal the strong box where the toll money was kept. He was seen by villagers and was eventually apprehended, tried for his crime and given the death sentence. After his execution, his body was left to hang in chains from a gibbet at Scrooby, near the scene of his crime, as a gruesome warning to other wrongdoers. His unquiet spectre is now said to haunt the area in the form of a man wearing a long black coat who stands beside the road for a while before fading away into the night…

OLLERTON, RUFFORD ABBEY c1955 O131016

FRANCIS FRITH

PIONEER VICTORIAN PHOTOGRAPHER

Francis Frith, founder of the world-famous photographic archive, was a complex and multi-talented man. A devout Quaker and a highly successful Victorian businessman, he was philosophical by nature and pioneering in outlook. By 1855 he had already established a wholesale grocery business in Liverpool, and sold it for the astonishing sum of £200,000, which is the equivalent today of over £15,000,000. Now in his thirties, and captivated by the new science of photography, Frith set out on a series of pioneering journeys up the Nile and to the Near East.

INTRIGUE AND EXPLORATION

He was the first photographer to venture beyond the sixth cataract of the Nile. Africa was still the mysterious 'Dark Continent', and Stanley and Livingstone's historic meeting was a decade into the future. The conditions for picture taking confound belief. He laboured for hours in his wicker dark-room in the sweltering heat of the desert, while the volatile chemicals fizzed dangerously in their trays. Back in London he exhibited his photographs and was 'rapturously cheered' by members of the Royal Society. His reputation as a photographer was made overnight.

VENTURE OF A LIFE-TIME

By the 1870s the railways had threaded their way across the country, and Bank Holidays and half-day Saturdays had been made obligatory by Act of Parliament. All of a sudden the working man and his family were able to enjoy days out, take holidays, and see a little more of the world.

With typical business acumen, Francis Frith foresaw that these new tourists would enjoy having souvenirs to commemorate their days out. For the next thirty years he travelled the country by train and by pony and trap, producing fine photographs of seaside resorts and beauty spots that were keenly bought by millions of Victorians. These prints were painstakingly pasted into family albums and pored over during the dark nights of winter, rekindling precious memories of summer excursions. Frith's studio was soon supplying retail shops all over the country, and by 1890 F Frith & Co had become the greatest specialist photographic publishing company in the world, with over 2,000 sales outlets, and pioneered the picture postcard.

FRANCIS FRITH'S LEGACY

Francis Frith had died in 1898 at his villa in Cannes, his great project still growing. By 1970 the archive he created contained over a third of a million pictures showing 7,000 British towns and villages.

Frith's legacy to us today is of immense significance and value, for the magnificent archive of evocative photographs he created provides a unique record of change in the cities, towns and villages throughout Britain over a century and more. Frith and his fellow studio photographers revisited locations many times down the years to update their views, compiling for us an enthralling and colourful pageant of British life and character.

We are fortunate that Frith was dedicated to recording the minutiae of everyday life. For it is this sheer wealth of visual data, the painstaking chronicle of changes in dress, transport, street layouts, buildings, housing and landscape that captivates us so much today, offering us a powerful link with the past and with the lives of our ancestors.

Computers have now made it possible for Frith's many thousands of images to be accessed almost instantly. The archive offers every one of us an opportunity to examine the places where we and our families have lived and worked down the years. Its images, depicting our shared past, are now bringing pleasure and enlightenment to millions around the world a century and more after his death.

For further information visit: www.francisfrith.com

INTERIOR DECORATION

Frith's photographs can be seen framed and as giant wall murals in thousands of pubs, restaurants, hotels, banks, retail stores and other public buildings throughout Britain. These provide interesting and attractive décor, generating strong local interest and acting as a powerful reminder of gentler days in our increasingly busy and frenetic world.

FRITH PRODUCTS

All Frith photographs are available as prints and posters in a variety of different sizes and styles. In the UK we also offer a range of other gift and stationery products illustrated with Frith photographs, although many of these are not available for delivery outside the UK – see our web site for more information on the products available for delivery in your country.

THE INTERNET

Over 100,000 photographs of Britain can be viewed and purchased on the Frith web site. The web site also includes memories and reminiscences contributed by our customers, who have personal knowledge of localities and of the people and properties depicted in Frith photographs. If you wish to learn more about a specific town or village you may find these reminiscences fascinating to browse. Why not add your own comments if you think they would be of interest to others? See **www.francisfrith.com**

PLEASE HELP US BRING FRITH'S PHOTOGRAPHS TO LIFE

Our authors do their best to recount the history of the places they write about. They give insights into how particular towns and villages developed, they describe the architecture of streets and buildings, and they discuss the lives of famous people who lived there. But however knowledgeable our authors are, the story they tell is necessarily incomplete.

Frith's photographs are so much more than plain historical documents. They are living proofs of the flow of human life down the generations. They show real people at real moments in history; and each of those people is the son or daughter of someone, the brother or sister, aunt or uncle, grandfather or grandmother of someone else. All of them lived, worked and played in the streets depicted in Frith's photographs.

We would be grateful if you would give us your insights into the places shown in our photographs: the streets and buildings, the shops, businesses and industries. Post your memories of life in those streets on the Frith website: what it was like growing up there, who ran the local shop and what shopping was like years ago; if your workplace is shown tell us about your working day and what the building is used for now. Read other visitors' memories and reconnect with your shared local history and heritage. With your help more and more Frith photographs can be brought to life, and vital memories preserved for posterity, and for the benefit of historians in the future.

Wherever possible, we will try to include some of your comments in future editions of our books. Moreover, if you spot errors in dates, titles or other facts, please let us know, because our archive records are not always completely accurate—they rely on 140 years of human endeavour and hand-compiled records. You can email us using the contact form on the website.

Thank you!

For further information, trade, or author enquiries
please contact us at the address below:

**The Francis Frith Collection, 6 Oakley Business Park,
Wylye Road, Dinton, Wiltshire SP3 5EU.**
Tel: +44 (0)1722 716 376 Fax: +44 (0)1722 716 881
e-mail: sales@francisfrith.co.uk **www.francisfrith.com**